Big
and Small

Alex Lane

Character illustrations by Jon Stuart

OXFORD

This animal is big.

This animal is small.

This animal has big legs.

This animal has small legs.

This animal has big feet.

This animal has small feet.

This animal has big teeth.

This animal has small teeth.

This animal has a big tail.

This animal has a small tail.

11

bird

This animal has big wings.

This animal has small wings.

This animal has a big mouth.

This animal has a small mouth.

Big | Small